welcome to
the dance

the poetry can

First published in Great Britain in 2001 by Poetry Can, Unit 11, Kuumba Project, 20-22 Hepburn Road, Bristol BS2 8UD.

Edited by Hester Cockcroft and Lucy Hudson, Poetry Can.

Designed by Martin Chester.

ISBN: 0-9539234-1-X

Acknowledgements

Poetry Can would like to acknowledge the financial support of the following organisations: The Adult and Community Education Service at Bath and North East Somerset Council, Awards for All and South West Arts.

The greatest of thanks to all the poets.

welcome to the dance
an introduction

The poems in this book are the result of a project entitled Life Lines 2001, primarily funded by the Adult and Community Education Service of Bath and North East Somerset Council. The Service is committed to lifelong learning opportunities for everyone and has supported the production of this work through its Widening Participation Fund. The Service is delighted to be part of this exciting project.

Between January and April 2001, three poets worked with older and disabled people living in residential accommodation in the Bath and North East Somerset area. All three poets had worked with the same groups of people on previous Poetry Can projects.

Alyson Sarah Hallett worked with older people resident at Henrietta House in Bath. Alyson has published fiction with Virago and Serpent's Tail, drama on Radio 4 and poetry with Queriendo Press. For the past year she has been writer in residence at South West Arts, reading and publishing her work widely throughout the region. She is committed to collaborative practice and has been commissioned by stained glass designers and a stone carver to make public text-based works of art.

Sara-Jane Arbury worked with older people resident at Smallcombe House and Bridgemead, again in Bath. Sara-Jane has worked as writer-in-residence in Taunton, Bristol, Swindon, Worcester, Dublin and four Oxfordshire village shops. Widely published, she has performed her poetry on television, radio and racecourses; at arts centres, clubs and festivals; in restaurants, schools and shopping malls. Sara-Jane co-hosts poetry slams around the country and programmes the Voices Off events at Cheltenham Festival of Literature.

Rosalyn Chissick worked with disabled people resident at the Greenhill House Cheshire Home in Timsbury near Midsomer Norton. Rosalyn is an award-winning novelist, poet and journalist. She has written two novels, Catching Shellfish Between the Tides, and colourbook, both published by Hodder and Stoughton. Her journalism is published in national newspapers and magazines. Rosalyn is currently writing her third novel.

contents

we say to the world

dreams

dreams
continued

just because we are not eye to eye

we say to the world

the sea

barbara burris

Cornwall
still wild in many places

no day trippers

walk the cliffs
and wander

think my own thoughts
and talk to no-one

rough waves
coming in over rock

I stand on the beach
look out to sea

the sea comes right into me
and gradually I feel contented

princes street gardens, edinburgh

peggy watson

trees, green grass
little hillocks

on one side of the street big shops
on the other, gardens

it makes you think
god was good
giving us grass and flowers

yellow daffodils

gardens all the length of the street

music

peggy watson, olive parker
barbara burris

music takes me to the sea
music takes me to dreamland
music takes me into the sunset

music takes you everywhere
music takes you where you want to go

music takes me not to the places
where it used to take me
unfortunately

the optimist

peggy watson

Thank god I'm healthy
I've lived a good long life
I'm ninety three
and hope to have another ninety three

So I'll be one hundred and eighty six
the next time I see you!

one shoe

barbara burris

I
remember
losing
a
shoe

I
remember
rushing
off
the
train
and
losing
a
shoe
on
the
tracks
of
Paddington
Station

I
remember
losing
a
shoe
and
walking
home
with
one
shoe
on
and
one
shoe

you never know how things can change

doris harler

You never know how things can change:
On a train to London there were no seats left.
I was standing in the aisle
and overheard two men saying they were getting of
at Chippenham.
I turned to the woman next to me and said:
"We'll have a seat soon."

The men got off
and the woman and I sat down
next to each other.
We talked all the way to Paddington
and, having enjoyed each other's company,
exchanged addresses.

I continued my journey to Spain
and when I returned to London two weeks later
made contact again.
We became good friends -
introduced each other to each other's friends
and family.
Within one year I was engaged to one of her cousins.

We were married for years
and I always remained grateful
to that fateful day when there were no seats left
on the Paddington train.

poetry

alyson sarah hallet

1

it's a song in my blood, poetry
it's a tree in my heart, rhyme
it's a fine day in winter, rhythm
it's a song in my blood, poetry

2

it's a lost love affair coming to life
it's one thousand views I thought I'd never see again
Westminster Bridge, Camelot, The Lake Isle of Innisfree
it's a song in my blood poetry

3

it's the song in my blood
it's the beat in my heart
it's the warmth of the sun
it's the light of the moon
it's the salt of the sea
it's the pulse of the free
it's a song in my blood
poetry

quotes

olive parker

"Life for us,
in that period,
was poetry itself."

hester cockcroft

"You're born to die:
it's what you do
in-between that matters."

olive parker

"I have led a wasted life:
so much I could have
done and didn't."

building bridges

alyson sarah hallett

There is an old woman
who seems impossibly young
in her purple shirt and moss-green skirt.

She is ninety six
and quick to move mind and body
even though her eyes are blind.

I sit next to her
and her soft, bony hand reaches for mine,
making contact before the stories begin.

She takes me to India
takes me to Spain
takes me to the street in London

Where she bought poetry with money
that should have been spent
on food or clothes or something essential.

Life for us in that period
was poetry itself, she says.
Then she quickly adds

I pray to be taken.
I pray to be taken, she says again, what use am I here
what use am I now?

building bridges

continued

There are twelve women sitting in this room
each one a volume unto herself
in a library that has never been read.

It's not your time, I say.
Why not, she asks, why not?
I don't know.

That's a lie. I do know.
Your stories change my life, I say.
She thinks for a moment then says,
That's very kind of you.

No, I say, not kind but true.
She looks at me with her blind eyes.
Do you really mean that? Yes.

She grips my hand tighter
and somewhere between us
there is a bridge.

Her life, my life,
a way for the old stories
to cross from one country to another

Bringing with them wit, wisdom, spirit;
her words walking into my living bones
rather than the dank, silent mud of a grave.

mount etna

barbara burris

You'd be standing looking

Seeing smoke
and fire

sparks
coming from the volcano

a feeling of awe
to stand and see
a mountain erupting

for years after
I'd lie in bed
and see it again

I forget now which husband
I went with

lakeland

nan still

We had a hotel
on Windermere Lake

A big garden and greenhouse,
a boat on the water

I used to play violin —

I've lived a good life
and good memories
mean more to me
than anything else

who it happens to

nan still

I was burned in the cradle:
a spark flew out the fire

the sadness on my mother's face
would make you weep

but it didn't make me weep
as it was me it happened to

.

---

welcome to the dance

mobile home

nan still

We used to put our caravan
on a train
– it was marvellous

we had a bath in it
a cooker –
it was a home.

We went all over the world in it – we met lots of
 little children.

They were always pleased to see us
– we didn't know why – couldn't understand a
word they said.

the moon

paul golf, graham du-plessis, stephen craig
(volunteers from king edward's school)

A torch in the sky

a beacon in darkness
dancing upon the shadowy hills

Moon lighting the sky at night
singing a song
dropping its moon magic

on Earth.

devastating no.1

various poets

Nobody knows
what happens
after death

Nobody knows
what another
is thinking

The Unknown is Devastating –

But some things
we aren't meant to know

Some things
are meant to be mysterious

Then there's always something to search for –

devastating no.2

various poets

When you're young and a boyfriend doesn't call
it's devastating

When you're older you just think
get another one!

the field

ruby sergeant

In a village close to Leicester
Stands a row of houses neat
Dignified, they lie
well sheltered from the noises of the street

For nigh on twenty years we lived there
Happy, smiling and serene
Viewing from our bedroom window
Just a country farmyard scene

In a sand-pit filled with water
Happy children came to fish
Swim and sail their rubber dinghys
For greater peace one could not wish

At the friendly game of cricket
Many a happy hour was spent
A thousand balls lost in the thicket
As the summer came and went

Through two world wars
We managed to survive both cool and calm
It took progress and its bombshell
To destroy our rural charm

the field

continued

Came the cry for houses
Houses! Rush them up no matter where
Turn the farmers from the r holdings
Houses! Houses everywhere

Hear the workmen's ribalc laughter
As their building tools they wield
See the snorting yellow monster
Churning up our lovely field

Gone our sandpit filled with water
Gone our shady, graceful trees
Gone our field, that children's playground
Progress scoffs at such as these

Bricks and mortar now surround us
Time goes on and old we grow
But nothing can erase the memory
Of the field we used to know.

untitled

ruby sergeant

P.C. Claxton went last Autumn
Out to watch his first post-mortem
Saw the entrails of a lady
Who died in circumstances shady

After seeing what was in her
He didn't feel a bit like dinner
Arriving home he gave a shiver
His landlady had cooked him liver.

He did not wish to hurt her feelings
So mixed it with potato peeling
And opening up the dustbin
Surreptitiously slipped it in

(And went off marching down the street)
Prepared to pound another beat
Most unfortunate for him
The dustbin lid made quite a din

His landlady woke from her sleep
In the bin she chanced to peep
When she saw her liver wailed,
Thinking her culinary arts had failed,

untitled

continued

"My lovely liver is not tasted"
She could not bear to see it wasted
She picked it up from where it fell
Dusted it and washed it well

And warmed it up, willy-nilly,
Served it up to her son Billy
Who ate it all with ravenous haste
Not a mouthful did he waste
Not even a morsel for the cat,
That then is the end of that.

But there's a moral to this story:
If you should survey a scene that's gory
Warn whoever cooks the dish
That you've a preference for fish!

reflections

ruby sergeant, alyson sarah hallett

The book I can't open is inside my head
It's permanently closed, I wish I was dead
It's full of long stories
And memories gone
I think of them all when I'm lying in bed.

I open the window and let in the moon
Twilight has gone, 'twill be dark very soon
Night owls are calling
Turn out the light
The time has come to leave this spirited room.

I go amongst the trees
And stretch my perishing knees
I dance with the stars
I walk above Mars
I look down at the world and what do I see?

I see the world smiling at me.

blues

ruby sergeant

I never felt more like singing the blues
Every time I watch the news
It's football,
It's got me singing the blues.

Whenever I turn on the telly at night
I get the picture clear and bright
It's football,
It's got me singing the blues.

It really drives me up the pole
To see them kiss when they score a goal
There's nothing left for me to do
But write this song and sing it to you.

Why don't sports have a channel of their own
Leave our favourite soaps alone
I tell you, it's got me singing the blues.

a time to...

barbara burris, sysie james
peggy watson, olive parker
ruby sergeant, doris harler

A time to think
A time to work
A time to play
And a most important time to pray

A time to speak
A time to seek
A time to sleep
And very often a time for silence

A time to wander
A time to ponder
A time for healing
A time for stealing on tip-toe to the
fridge in the middle of the night

A time to grow
A time to flow
A time to walk
And a time to go

you've only got one life
barbara burris

You've Only Got One Life
Be Confident To Do The Things You Want
Don't Listen To Other's Doubts
You've Only Got One Life
Grab It!

we say to the world...
ruby sergeant, olive parker, peggy watson, sysie james

Live Life and Laugh
Live Life and Love
Live Life and Look Around For Bargains

Pray: with sincerity

Love: with sincerity

Live Happily and Love Each Other

prayer

ruby sergeant, olive parker

Prayers and Action –
   the world needs both

You need Prayer
   to make you do the right action

Prayer and Faith
   the world needs both

It Wouldn't Be a Right Prayer Without Faith
   it would just be words

Life is Very Strange
   it makes you wonder what death is like

Everything Depends On
   how deeply you believe, how deeply you feel

the magic steam train arrives at 33 henrietta street, bath

ruby sergeant, doris harler, olive parker, nan still, peggy watson, barbara burris, evie philips, sysie james, alyson sarah hallett

a steam train's
the only train for me
the slower it goes
the more you see

a steam train
arrives at number thirty three
anyone can go anywhere
completely for free

a steam train's
the only train for me
the slower it goes
the more you see

We've got two for Eastbourne
Two for India
One for Edinburgh
One for Australia

welcome to the dance

There's one for San Francisco
One for Cornwall
One for the West Indies
One who's changed her mind to Malta

a steam train's
the only train for me
the slower it goes
the more you see

Now there's only one left
and she's going all the way
travelling around the world
for a year and a day

a steam train's
the only train for me
the slower it goes
the more you see

something abides

alyson sarah hallett

call it heart
call it soul
its essence is whole
its nature is peace

beyond the tide
beyond the moon
something abides
something abides

like water we change
like water we change
cloud, steam, sea, rain,
rain, steam, sea

something abides
something abides
in the endless chain
of endless change

something free abides

welcome to the dance

dreams

poetry

grace walton

Is something
You leave
On the page
As you live

I remember, I remember when queen victoria died

alice barter

I remember, I remember
When Queen Victoria died

Everybody wore black
Black armbands

Even the milkman
Who came to the door

With warm milk
Straight from the cow

The light from the lamp post already out
As the day's darkness dawned

all daddy was to me

betty allday

All Daddy was to me
Was a picture
And when he came back
From the war
I said "Hello Grandpa"

day dreams

grace walton

Combing out my hair
Dreaming of primroses in the damp earth
Warmer days and lighter nights
Walking in the woods at mid-day
Birds busy building nests – it's Spring

Soon the days will be busy with crops
Harvesting apples
Seeing old friends
Talking of past adventures
Being twenty-five again

Combing out my hair
Only remembering happy times
Recalling beautiful landscapes
And the people walking there

when you're old

nell lewis

When you're old
It's amazing to me
How often
Your friends and relatives
Appear to you in your dreams
It's lovely to see them all
When you're old

dreaming – what is that

grace glover

Dreaming – what is that
Once we are fast asleep?
Is it wishful thinking
Of places we would seek?

It need not be just places
As people come in too
It could turn out a nightmare
Especially if it's of you

alice barter (b. 1896): congratulations on reaching your hundredth birthday

sara-jane arbury

It was just an ordinary card
Not even from the Queen
Just a secretary
– The Home Secretary
I think it was –

I was disappointed

1896 - 1969

sara-jane arbury

The seventy-three years between Alice and me
Sit in a chair with a cup of tea
And adjusts her hearing-aid to the talk
Of the here and now and what happened before
The Suffragettes, trams, eclipses of the moon
The Internet, emails and mobile phones
And she stares as if looking through water in a glass
At the time of her life bending the future to the past
This invisible woman aged seventy-three
As young as a centenarian and as old as me

I must go back to barbados again

evan alleyne

I must go back to Barbados again
To coconut vendors and memories of youth
And all I ask is to sail on The Bajan Queen
To the Salvation Army and William Booth

I must go back to Barbados again
Parliament Buildings, cricket and flying fish
And all I ask is to smell the hibiscus
And sample Sam Lord's Castle Dish

I must go back to Barbados again
To Independence Arch and Black Rock
And all I ask is to bind all hearts
With a pride that doesn't boast or mock

I must go back to Barbados again
To family, steel bands and Limbo
And all I ask is to surf the wind
And gaze at Gun Hill from my window

I must go back to Barbados again
If only to hear our Anthem's choir
Singing in one voice throughout the land
With Our Lord to guide and inspire

welcome to the dance

Singing:
We loyal sons and daughters all
Do hereby make it known
These fields and hills beyond recall
Are now our very own

We write our names on history's page
With expectations great
Strict guardians of our heritage
Firm craftsmen of our fate

(Note: The last time I saw Barbados was in 1948)

dreaming
the day away
margaret stone

Ringing for help first thing in the morning
Dreaming of being able-bodied and planning
my day's future

Changing my calendar as soon as I get out of bed
Dreaming of business dates and birthdays

Drinking a cup of coffee made by the volunteers
Dreaming of retirement work in the local hospital

Listening to the radio according to what's on
Dreaming of classical music I heard long ago

Telephoning my friends in the evening
Knowing that's my life-line

I'm dreaming of opening the innings for england

bill burden

I'm dreaming of opening the innings for England
Walking out through the gates at Lords
For once, the weather's fine
A packed house, thirty thousand or so
Walking out onto the pitch
Nerves a-jangle, nerves on edge
Must succeed, must succeed
So many have failed at this stage
I mustn't fail...

On the pitch now, taking guard
A feeling of elation – I'm in charge
The cricket bat in my hand
Is a weapon that gives me power
And yes!
The first four!
The crowd are on their feet
Cheering me on – I did it!

Relaxing now the first four has been made
My thoughts wander back over the years
To great batsmen of the past
Hobbs, Sutcliffe, Compton, Botham
They're all in the pavilion
Watching me making my run
And now in my mind's eye
I'm one of them

ninety not out

gwen rowland

My chief dream was marriage
And the baby became my life
I was certainly kept busy
Working as mother and wife

My husband though took ill
We couldn't socialise much
I also looked after my mother
And felt out of touch

As I didn't go out in the evening
So all I did was knit
But now I wear my cardigan
And here is where I sit

what is this life if...

kate haffner

Sitting here in my armchair
Sitting here with the time to stare
My mind drifts back to my late husband
And of the time the washing machine broke down

He told me not to worry about it
Said "On Monday we'll get a good one Kate"
I remember sorting the laundry out
And then off he went to the laundrette

And there at the laundrette, he dropped down dead
No-one contacted me, he didn't have his address
The doctor examined him for reasons why
But I thought what a good way for him to die

Sitting here in my armchair
Sitting here with the time to stare
My mind drifts back to my late husband
And of the time the washing machine broke down

psychic experience

Once I saw my brother
Who had died six months before
It was during an air raid
And the room was blacked out
Thick heavy curtains
Not a chink of light allowed
When suddenly a shape appeared
Right before my eyes
A bright fluorescent oval
Bit by bit becoming

Man-sized

And out of the oval
There came a young man
Looking handsome and smart
In a beautiful silver-grey suit
I said "Oh Stanley
How lovely to see you"
He threw back his head and laughed
I woke up my husband
Who said "It's only a dream"
But I never grieved again for him

48   welcome to the dance

outside while having a cigarette

rose leon

Outside while having a cigarette
I often see animal life lurking in the pavement
In the pattern of raindrops drying out
I spy a huge tiger, two bright eyes, roaring mouth
And sometimes as I gaze up high at the trees
I pick out a duck in the shape of the leaves

I usually see animals, big cats on the ground
And feel lovely in myself that no-one else notices
them padding around
They don't seem to see the funny things that I see
When my dreams come creeping up quietly on me
Weaving their way through the patterns of the carpets
Or hidden in the prints of other people's footsteps

when I was ten

grace walton

When I was ten
And life expanded
I learned to leapfrog
The jerk upwards
Surmounting the body
Making the landing
I never got stuck

Overcoming all obstacles
Placed in my way
Researching the ins and outs
The ups and downs of life
Looking for leads in ideas
And learning as I go along
More of a challenge this way

If there are five men in a fishing boat
Who are these people?
Where have they come from?
What are their origins?
When you look at a person
What do you see?
A past? A future?
Or simply the present?

as we sit here writing poems
grace glover

As we sit here writing poems
Thinking what to say
The sun is shining brightly
It is a smashing day

The ideas come too slowly
The mind has gone a blank
I think I now realise
I'm as thick as a plank

day dreams

evan alleyne

Having a shower at half past seven
Dreaming of Barbados, blue sea, sunshine and
friendliness

Eating my breakfast on my own in comfort
Dreaming of rice, split peas, meal corn cuckoo and
whole pea soup

Carrying out my devotions without any interruptions
Dreaming of visiting St. Stephen's Boys School again

Going to the Senior Citizens' Club
Dreaming of Carrington's Village, Eagle Hall,
Waverley Avenue and Bridgetown

Listening to 'Sailing By' on Radio 4
Dreaming of hearing the Barbadian accent once more

untitled

sara-jane arbury

The woman who's a hundred and two
Is bundled in blankets and having a snooze

She used to work as a seamstress in London
The Queen Mother came in every now and again

Her fingers have become pins and needles of bone
She drifts into dreams where she's all on her own

"Has everyone gone?" She wakes with a cry
And feels a pat on her hand in reply

I wish I was young again

grace glover

I wish I was young again
And walked about with ease
I would revisit places
That in the past had pleased

The district of my childhood
As a teenager I roamed
The miles that I cycled
Far away from home

Then I got married
Moved to a different home
Oh how I'd love to go back
And round those places roam

in the middle of the night

nell lewis

I must have had a dream last night
Because I heard someone quite distinctly
Say   my   name

It was a lady's voice
Not a man's
And it made me think of my mother

She woke me up as she had done so before
But the room was pitch-black as always
And no-one was there

nothing there

bill burden

Since my time in hospital
Everything seems so real
I journey to America
Every night on a plane
And when I wake up
After hours of flight
I'm back in my bed again

Each morning I see from my window
A valley and in the distance, a hill
With motorbikes, cattle and vehicles
Lorries and sometimes a horse
Moving on down
Towards my room
As if it's a matter of course

Or else I see boys playing
Rugby, cricket or corps activity
Always wearing similar shirts
Even when dressed for war
I go on seeing them
Day after day
My dreams are real, I'm sure

the reality of dreams

pat ricketts

My older brother went to Cambridge
And I remember when I was quite small
He told me about the theory of relativity
"What you expect to find here is really
somewhere else"
A bit like me I suppose
Here, there, always elsewhere

I always wanted a baby brother or sister

margaret stone

I always wanted a baby brother or sister
I was the youngest and d dn't know why
My school friends had baby brothers and sisters
But I just didn't get any

I prayed every night for baby brothers or sisters
In the way we were taught in those days
My dolls were my baby brothers and sisters
But still I didn't get any

I trained as a nanny and worked with mothers and
their children
Never married, had none of my own
Spent too much of my time with mothers and their
children
And for me, they just didn't come

Because I was always with mothers and their children
I never met up with the opposite sex
I gave up my youth to mothers and their children
So for me, they just didn't come

The war came and mothers waved off their children
All the young ones were called up
I worked in a shop, became too old for children
That was the way it worked out

The job wasn't easy, old men, no children
Life was difficult during the war
Eighty-four now, no husband, no children
But that's just the way it worked out

highs and lows

nell lewis

When I was little
I sang my first solo
"Just A Little Sunbeam
Shining On Its Way'"
At the Sunday School chapel

I was such a little sunbeam
That they stood me on a stage
Of books and Bibles
To make me taller
But I was bright for my age

At school my voice took me higher
I won a prize for my soprano
I remember the girl who won contralto
Was called Olive Naylor
Eighty years ago

there was an old lady from bath spa

sara-jane arbury

There was an old lady from Bath Spa
Who made an unfortunate birthday faux pas
As her candles burned brightly
She blew them so sprightly
Her dentures nearly travelled afar

there was an old lady from leeds

nell lewis

There was an old lady from Leeds
Who grew all her flowers from seeds
She worked hard and long
Even sang them a song
As she'd heard that they'd really be pleased

At the show at Devizes
She won lots of prizes
This green-fingered lady from Leeds

guessing game

sara-jane arbury

How old am I?
Eighty-eight I reply
No eighty-four
Please don't make me any older
Old age comes quick enough already
My dear

dream list

evan alleyne

As a Senior Citizen
My dreams are of simple things

Relaxation
Good health
Peace of mind
Finance without worry, not riches
Loyal friends and how to be one
Wisdom and understanding my prayer
To be able to forgive and be forgiven
To be wanted or missed

As a Senior Citizen
My dreams are of simple things

the carer

grace glover

Whose buzzer is that buzzing?
What do they want right now?
Shall I pretend that I've gone deaf?
I would love to – and how

I don't suppose it's urgent
It seldom is you know
"Please can I have a tissue?"
Is how it usually goes

My feet are really killing me
I'd love a cup of tea
But a voice is calling from afar
"Please someone come and help me"

There are baths to do and necks to wash
It really is a bore
And five o'clock is a long way off
So on I plod once more

So keep on with the buzzer
I'm coming with brush and comb
On second thoughts I've changed my mind
I think I'll just go home

welcome to the dance

the bliss of soltiude...

sara-jane arbury

Pat sits in his chair
And wanders lonely as a cloud
Here and there

Back to The Lakes, the vales and hills
He's with his daughter
Searching for daffodils

He sees them now, though he didn't before
"August. Wrong time of year.
They weren't there any more."

memorable equation

nell lewis

Two parents +
Two brothers +
Two sisters +
Two husbands =
One life

here to there

evan alleyne

I remember, I remember
Eagle Hall, the area where I was born
The policeman in black and white on a box
Street traders selling roast corn
The smell of baking bread

I remember, I remember
St. Stephen's Boys School, C of E
Teachers well-dressed, all male
At assembly we sang with glee
"I salute the flag, the mighty Empire!"

I remember, I remember
Those days I was running wild
The sugar cane, corn on the cob
I was my mother's only child
Sometimes happy, other times sad

I remember, I remember
The Church and all it meant
Learning to swim or play cricket
To my Gran and two Aunts I went
A rescue in time of need

I remember, I remember
Three lovely maidens fair
The smell of apple blossoms
Oh, the laughter and the cheer
A daughter, a wife, a home

I remember, I remember
Barbados, I knew you then
Oh, the memories of my youth
To return I know not when
My thanks to you

this morning at the dentist's
barbara caney

This morning at the dentist's
Lying outstretched on the bed
My mind climbed mountainsides
In Norway with the Girl Guides

Next I travelled to Germany
Where the buildings are so big
My father was happy to send me
With the people from the Army

From there to Weston-super-Mare
Ice cream, buckets and spades
A school trip for a day in the sun
Sandcastles and lots of fun

This morning at the dentist's
Lying outstretched on the bed
While he was searching for decay
I was elsewhere, far, far away

causley's contemporaries

sara-jane arbury

I saw a jolly pensioner
With a jolly pen
Writing a jolly poem
With jolly acumen.

But soon jolly pensioner
Out of jolly luck.
Hits jolly writer's block.
Words jolly stuck.

Jolly poem jolly dead
Cut down in jolly prime.
Should jolly poetry
Jolly well rhyme?

There is no jolly answer
Said the jolly Muse.
Just follow where I jolly go –
You cannot jolly lose.

Jolly pensioner has to run.
Muse is jolly fast.
But soon on jolly paper
The final jolly verse at last.

In jolly voice and jolly style
The jolly poem's read.
Jolly glad I've written that.
Jolly good, I said.

just because we are
not eye to eye

don't watch the size

stephen macpherson

Just because we're not eye to eye
Doesn't mean we can't be of the same stature
I've known a couple of very short people but
They were bigger than me spiritually.

Such people's presence exploded with
an effervescence.

the face

dawn clipson

Itchy feet
warm legs
bony knees
squashy bottom
empty stomach
bony ribs
soft arms
bony shoulders
warm neck
bony forehead
soft hair
warm ears
bony nose
soft lips
bony chin
bony cheeks
open eyes

multiple sclerosis - my feelings

viv waller

I noticed my feet felt heavy when I walked and I could no longer dance. My doctor treated me for fallen arches but they were not improving, so he sent me to a specialist who made me walk across the floor without my shoes. He said he didn't like the way I was walking and would I go into hospital for a week under observation.

When in hospital the first thing was a brain scan to confirm I did not have a tumour or other trouble. They took blood from my arm every day then made me hold objects in my closed hand and tell them what they were, finally I had a lumbar puncture.

The doctor did not tell me what he thought was wrong but I had to go back in a month and by then I was dragging my left foot. I was then told it was M.S.

There were tears at first as I realised that I would never be able to do the things I loved doing most, long walks and dancing, then I was angry. What had I done to deserve this, why me? Then after a lot of thought I was determined to fight it and make the most of what I could do. After all nobody wants to know you if you are miserable all of the time.

My son and daughter had both been married only a couple of years, so I did not want to put the responsibility of looking after me on to either of them, so elected to go into a Home. My Doctor suggested a Cheshire Home and, as there was one near my daughter who lived in Bath, I applied and was accepted. I have been at Timsbury Home for 21 years.

acting

barbara vaughan

I was an actress
I had flu symptoms
I lay in bed.
I was living with a man
and I couldn't walk properly.
I used to hum 'rumpa-pa-pum'
as I clung onto his arm.
He was sympathetic but he left me
and got married.

And then a good friend
used to take me out on his motorbike.
I joined a theatre group in London
and was able to carry on working.
I forgot about the illness
which had been diagnosed as M.S.

But occasionally it would affect my career
during one play I was unable to do the dance routine.
For me the worst moments have been
when I say I can do something
and then am unable to do it

Having to accept the fact that I could no longer walk
but had to go into a wheelchair.
This and losing my home
have been to my utmost horror
and far, far worse than any physical change.

I feel sad most of the time
and my sense of humour is slipping away from me.

may my pen be as sharp as the sword that cut my life to shreds

michael jacob

In the late seventies
I had a bad bird-like trip
which terminated
in a near-fatal return to earth.
I broke just one bone
my jaw bone
through which I entered a coma
that lasted three months.
My brain damage
led to the dissolution of that pearl beyond price
our marriage.
At the time of my hang-gliding crash
our sons
Dan and Barney
were aged six and three
and our daughter Zoe
was less than a year old.
Their mother did great things for them
raising each with great love
and with great good sense.
Now all three have reached adulthood
bless them
but where is there room
in the lives of those four
for a disabled ex-husband and father?

dawn remembers

dawn clipson

I remember running home from school
and dancing to bands
Joe Loss at university.
I was wearing a dark blue velvet dress
my hair was curly
gold shoes
big hall
paper decorations, red and green.
I was dancing with my husband
then boyfriend, John
ballroom dancing

I remember cooking rock cakes
and fish and chips, pancakes and
potatoes in their jackets and sponge cakes

I remember walking over the hills with mummy
the grass was tall
there were bluebells
cornflowers, primroses and cowslips
It was a warm summer's day
I was wearing a dress with pink spots
I remember green grass

I remember tea, bread, butter and jam
at home
in the dining room
with mummy
there was a blue tablecloth

It's nice to remember
I feel warm inside
I can't do those things now
how sad.

becoming disabled isn't easy

anne wilson

My parents knew they might have a disabled child as my mother had Muscular Dystrophy. These days doctors can do tests on embryos but, unfortunately, they didn't have the technology then that they do now. Like many women, my mother wanted a child more than anything in the world, even if it meant putting a child's life in danger. The consequences were dramatic.

When I was two years old, my mother became ill and sadly died of pneumonia. She was only 31. She left a young father and her baby daughter on their own. That was in late January 1979. By April of the same year, my father remarried, giving me a brother and sister and, most of all, a new mother. A year later my step mum gave birth to a son and, when he was two, we moved to South Africa where we spent six and a half wonderful years.

The first time my parents noticed something was wrong was when I started running. My legs drifted off to the sides. At school, I noticed other children laughed at me when I ran or talked. Mum and dad gave me the best upbringing they could, but they knew they couldn't hide the fact I had a disability for ever. They knew that one day I'd start asking questions.

The first time I noticed my disability was at a school sports day. We had to do this dance routine and, as the music started, I found I couldn't get up off the

becoming disabled
isn't easy
continued

grass. In the end, a teacher helped me up and gave me a chair and the dance began again. At the time I thought nothing of it. I thought it was a one-off. I was wrong, very wrong.

By the time I was 10, M.D. had really taken its hold on me. I kept falling down and hitting my head. It really hurt. When we arrived back in England, mum and dad set about finding a school for disabled children. When I started attending the school in Stroud, Gloucestershire, I was able to walk into town, which was twenty minutes away. As the years went by I found it harder and harder. I was determined to walk there come hell or high water but, in the end, I gave in and started using a scooter the local golf club gave me. For holidays, the school gave me a wheelchair so I could go out with my family. It really was impossible to walk anywhere. I guess that's when I knew I was different.

Over the six years at school, I competed in many school sports events across the country, even appearing on TV, radio and in newspapers, sometimes to raise money for children in Africa and children with disabilities here in the UK. But I found I needed to use my chair more and more, even if it was just to go and see my sister who lived 200 yards down the road from mum and dad. I did manage to walk down to the pub on my 17th birthday with a few friends, but they had to carry me back to school. No, I wasn't drunk, I was just unable to make my legs work.

welcome to the dance

I left school with 4 G.C.S.E.s and a number of medals in sports and swimming. I was about to start my years of drinking, sleeping and pulling men - but sadly only two out of three happened. SHAME! After about two months, I was getting bored and decided to go and work at the local play group with the youngsters but sadly I had to stop as my disability was getting worse and I ended up in hospital more and more.

In '97 I went on holiday with the Wiltshire Red Cross. While dancing in my wheelchair on the last night, I fell out onto a wooden floor, hurting my head, hips, back and knees. I spent four weeks in hospital, but looking back three years on, I knew something was wrong. The day before going away, I got stuck on the toilet and cried as I was unable to move. In the end, dad came in and helped me off the loo. Also, while showering, I couldn't get in or out of the bath, so mum had to come in, calm me down and help me shower. This was the start of everybody's worst nightmare.

In '98, I was taken into hospital yet again with a chest infection. While there, I pulled a muscle in my left shoulder so doctors gave me Aspirin to ease the pain but I had an allergic reaction and was rushed into Royal United Hospital in Bath. Mum rang all her friends to pray for me to pull through, and they rang their friends. People all over the world prayed for me.

In '99, I ended up in hospital a number of times but they were never life threatening to me. They were chest infections and when I get an infection I feel

becoming disabled isn't easy

really bad and find it hard to breathe and eat and
drink. In 2000, everything was going fine up until my
nephew's birthday, when I got a really bad chest
infection and on Easter Monday, I was rushed into
hospital. If I had not been rushed in I would have
died. I hadn't eaten for about two weeks and drinking
anything was really hard. I was losing weight fast.
Then, on May 5th, I had an operation to fit a feeding
tube. It's taken away the joy of eating chocolate,
cake and all the things that are bad for you but I'm a
lot healthier and I'm putting on weight now. I've
always been five stone and now I'm about six stone.

I know my M.D. is getting worse but, in the year 2001,
I'm still here and I've just turned 24. I've been very
lucky to live this long and I'm hoping there's a few
more years left in me. I got to see in the 21st century
at least. I've had a good life and working with young
children has helped me and them to understand what
life really means. If there is one thing I know for sure,
it's the fact I've changed those children's lives for the
better as they will grow up knowing that everyone isn't
the same and hopefully they won't stare or laugh at
other children who are different to them. Even now, if
I'm in town and one of them sees me, they will come
up and give me a hug and say hi. I've made a
difference to those children's lives and my nieces and
nephews' lives because they'll grow up knowing some
people are different and I'm glad and proud of all the
children I've been around, because they can make a
difference in the future.

a bright blue chair

jenny quinn

No longer were running, strolling, dancing and
walking fun.
They had all become a thing of the past.

Ah, but the memories were still there.
Running away from boys one moment
Then dancing with them in the high life of the sixties.
Strolling through tall grasses hand in hand over three
continents.
Walking after children, doing the shopping, chores,
work commitments.

Then
Stumbling, swaying, dragging a leg or two.
Clutching at walls, one stick, then two.
One person and finally two to keep me upright.

What a relief when a bright blue chair came to my aid.
I learned to do wheelies.
Carried things on my lap.
Sat on a spongy comfortable cushion.
Propelled myself around on wheels.
I could reach things without falling over.
Save my strength to make witty remarks.
My friends who took me out got to park where
others couldn't.
I had a glass of red wine without my head falling off

Without my wheelchair I could not have had such fun.
My bright blue chair is an aid to mobility not
a sentence.
It gave me independence.

the loss of one's independence through wheelchair confinement

michael jacob

Regardless of one's past life experience, being the captive of a wheelchair renders the firm assertion of one's will virtually impossible.

Without eye to eye contact, one can no longer say 'boo to a goose' with convincing conviction.

From my own experience, when seated in a wheelchair, I have been regarded by both members of my family, and by friends, as not being fully intelligent. But the most vital effect of all is how wheelchair status directly affects one's whole lifestyle. As a free and, as yet, non-institutionalised being, this is surely bound up with having the financial resources to maintain one's own private home and one's family in it. For most people, myself included, such financial resources depend upon being employed. But convincing oneself, or a potential employer of one's suitability for such employment if a wheelchair captive, is far from easy. In my own case, unemployment led to divorce, loss of home and eventual banishment to a residential institution. C'est la vie with a vengeance.

life in a wheelchair
viv waller

After struggling to walk
holding onto furniture
for fear of falling
it was heaven
to get across the room
in safety
in a wheelchair.

what is your perception?
stephen macpherson

Disability can be whatever you want it to be,
it is up to you. It can be what people say it
is, which is what they see, or it can be what
you feel it is. You may even consider it non-
existent. I am not disabled. The path I'm
walking has enabled me to experience what
many can't even conceive. This whole life
is a roller coaster obstacle course, that's what
I believe - or rather feel - because I keep my
senses open a great deal.

encounters with
able bodied people
viv waller

How lucky they are
to be able to nip about
or even run
when it takes so long
to get about in a wheelchair
and it's so much effort.

They tell us how nice it would be
to sit down all day
but it gets very boring
sitting in one position.

I watch able bodied people move
with such ease and I envy them.

When I hear music I would love to dance
That is the thing I long for most.
Unless you have been static
you cannot realise what it is like.

If I want to give someone a hug
I have to wait for them to come to me.

still young at heart

phil hill

They say I'm able-bodied but that really isn't true
For the things accomplished in my youth they haven't got
a clue.
I was the pin-up strong man I could carry on at length
But now I feel frustrated for I know I've not
the strength.
I'll settle now for who I am with patched up
body parts;
But still I feel I'm capable of beating them at darts.
They say here comes the one-eyed chap with a black
patch on his eye;
He thinks he's going to beat us - suppose we'd better let
him try.
I know they say this all in fun; but imagine how I feel
Remembering vigorous days long since; this life now
seems unreal.
Our bodies are like cars - they need a service now
and then.
Some parts can be replaced to get us going
once again.
But there will surely come a time when they will have
to stop,
And common sense will say I must accept what I
have got.

blind or ignorant?

stephen macpherson

Some people have convenient deafness when it
comes to being asked 'excuse me' by someone in a
wheelchair.

Many times I've needed to tap or tug lightly on
someone's clothing to gain attention.
Some people grab their bags as if to protect them
from a thief or backing away from a monster.

Some people seem to think being in a wheelchair is
a disease.
Some people are afraid to come near you.
Some people stare blankly at you with an expression
saying: 'eurh, look at the poor soul.'

try - a message to able bodied people

anne wilson

Try being in a wheelchair for a day or two
Try going to the toilet when you want to.

Try going shopping on your own
Try getting into shops that have high steps.

Try going out for a meal with family or friends
Try getting under short tables or to the bar.

Try living a full and happy life
Try moaning about your problems, then think
about ours.

Try reaching up or down to get a book or a pair
of shoes
Try buying clothes that aren't designed for
the disabled.

Try going to a family or friends house, where they
have a step to enter
Try living in your own home with stairs and no help.

You see, there is more to being disabled than
people realise
Part of being disabled is leaning to cope at home and
out and about.

So please remember that no two people are the same
in their disabilities
So stop thinking your little problems are much bigger
than they really are

Thank you.

---

just because I'm in a wheelchair my dad doesn't care

stephen macpherson

Just because I'm in a wheelchair my dad doesn't care
He left me in his potato patch and told me to
stay there.
After a few hours of puffing and panting I had got all
the potatoes out.
Dad looked around to see if there were any other
jobs about.
'Ah there you go Stephen, here's a hoe, get rid of all
those weeds
Then go and rest. It better be a good job
Otherwise you won't get that chicken breast for tea.'

That afternoon I began to swoon in the summer heat
I had to stay on my feet - well in reality, upright in
my seat
Because I had to put the potatoes away nice
and neat.

my carers

jenny quinn

In there anyone more important to a disabled person
than a carer?
Society never values them.
Others see them as lowly workers.
They are underpaid.
Their contribution to society is never appreciated.
And yet
We who depend on them for our existence cannot do
without them.

Sometimes you meet one who outshines all others.
A remarkable woman.

I have two in my life, Shona and Kathy.

Shona, a name to be cherished
Who makes my day spring to light.
Whose compassion and caring allows me to sing with
joy.
Whose spirit and soul are truly inspirational.

Shona, my carer who looks after me.
Bathes me, dresses me.
Makes my bed.
Feeds me.
Cleans my flat.
Washes and irons my clothes.
Massages my legs when they ache with spasms.

Attends to my incontinent personal needs.
Never allows me to feel low.
Makes me laugh.
Feeds and cuddles my dog, Poppy, who adores her.
Cooks food fit for a queen.
Decorates my flat with flowers of every hue.
Gives me presents with meaning:
Lila Lamp who sits on my computer,
Telling me to keep writing.
A silver bracelet
Because she knows I love silver more than gold.
That reminds me of the moon and romance.

Shona
Who encourages me to reach my ultimate
achievements
Believes in me.

Shona
My carer and friend,
Who fills an empty space in my heart.

Kathy, who sees me five mornings a week.
Whose opening line to me every morning is
"Get out of that bed."

She runs my bath and bathes me.
Dresses me.
Makes my breakfast.
Reminds me to take my pills.
Changes the linen on my bed.
Hoovers the flat.
Dusts everywhere.

Kathy does my shopping and banking.
Takes Poppy to the doggy groomers.
Collects my pads from the hospital.
Arranges her roster to fit in my schedule.
Takes me for medical appointments.

She laughs at my stripy socks.
Then gets someone to knit me more.

Kathy, the ultimate carer.
Her actions speak louder than her words.
Quiet and unassuming.
Yet, with a sense of fun.
We tease each other.
And laugh a lot.

Kathy my carer and friend.
The rock my life depends on.

a personal realisation

stephen macpherson

Every time I say 'I can't' or 'that's too much for me,' I
remember times when my dad, physio or nurse said:
'you can' and in their presence somehow I did.
Today I just thought of them and it worked.

awful

dawn clipson

I miss my husband
my mother
my sister
Salisbury - my home.

At first I felt cross
now I accept being here
I've been here 26 years.

the bar

anne wilson

Down in the bar
In Greenhill House
Everyone's getting loud
Laughing and talking in a crowd

Drinking red wine
Some drinking coke and rum
Some drinking double Baileys too
All getting slightly drunk

Wheelchairs coming and going
Music on with people dancing
All singing out of tune

Goodness gracious me
There goes another diet Coke
All over the floor and me!

fact 1

stephen macpherson

As a matter of fact, I don't consider
myself disabled at all.
I may be in a chair but otherwise I'm
quite tall.

the green glass wall
rosalyn chissick

Carl is coming back. I've missed him. Waking each morning he is my first thought: Carl - where is he, how is he - is he thinking about me? Seven years since I saw him, touched his body, heard his voice. But in dreams I call and he comes to me.

"Saphy," he says, "Saphy, I'm over here."

7 a.m. Light filters in through the curtains. I have so much to do. I lay here warm, uneasy, excited. Reluctant to leave the sheets. In the room next door I can hear Millie moving around. Her voice reciting the names of her toys. Ticking them off like her teacher with the register: Maisie, Puffin, Carolyn, Lou.

I reach onto the floor for leggings and a T-shirt. Yesterday's knees left saggy imprints in the cloth and today's knees appear smaller, neater. What will he think of me? Seven years. In the mirror I imagine I can see every day etched onto my face. I had a different look about me then. So much has changed.

And nothing. The flat we shared - same curtains and carpets, same TV, Frieda's cups and plates. I remember the day she presented them to us. Carl stormed out. Got back in the early hours and we sat up smoking, drinking. He told me he was sorry. We made love in the early morning. It was one of the last times.

welcome to the dance

Carl is coming home. I have a letter to prove it. I've been carrying it around in my pocket. I sleep with it by my head.

I meet Millie in the kitchen. She has Puffin under one arm. He is green and blue with one wobbly eye. She is wearing one of Carl's old T-shirts. It reaches her knees.

"It's a special day," I remind her. "Carl is coming back."

She sits cross legged in the green armchair eating Coco Pops. Puffin sits beside her. The radio is on.

"Saturday the ninth of October," the presenter says. "Cloud in the early part of the day, then sunshine."

I lie back in steam and bubbles and imagine Carl's hands on me. He is the white foam, the hot water, the vanilla soap stroking my skin. I dunk my head under the water. It gives me a feeling of timelessness. It can be as if he never went away. We can go back.

Standing up now on the rough white rug we bought in Greece. Rubbing my body dry. I have been deciding what to wear for over a week. Since Carl's letter arrived, his homecoming has been all there is. Jeans and a red T-shirt. He doesn't like make-up, dislikes fussiness. I wear trainers and lip-coloured lipstick.

Then we sit in the lounge. Millie and I. The TV is

blaring and the clock's hands go round. At midday I make us both a cheese sandwich. By 2 p.m. I've picked all the clear polish off my nails and I am starting to bite my fingers. Angry red skin at the sides of my nails.

Millie says: "I thought Carl was coming."

And I say: "we must be patient."

Then there is a knock at the door and hot quick tears fill my eyes. I stand up. My knees are water. My legs move towards Carl but I can't feel them. My heart is banging in my ears, it hurts my chest. I open the door and a woman stands there.

"Saphy."

The woman says my name a few times before I hear her. She is wearing jeans. Her hair is dark.

"Saphy."

Only one person has ever called me Saphy. The woman reaches across the gap between us.

"Saphy, it's me."

I want to slam the door. I want this person to disappear forever. I want to scream and cry and kick and bite.

Millie is pulling on my leg. Her eyes are the same as the strangers. Big and round and full of fear. I do not have words. I do not have anything.

The stranger has dropped to her knees. She is looking past my legs to Millie.

"Hello," she says. "I have a present for you."

"What is it?" Millie asks.

The stranger is sitting in our lounge on the green armchair asking Millie questions.

"How old are you?"

"Seven."

"Do you go to school?"

Millie has undone the package with the yellow ribbon and, while she gives mumbled answers, she is studying her new doll. She has long black hair. Her body is smooth and shiny. The box says her name is Roxanne and she wants to be our friend.

I watch the stranger's busy fingers. The way they keep touching her face and earrings. As if to reassure herself that she is all still there.

"This must be a shock," she says at last and turns her face towards me.

I know that face, those eyes, that mouth. I stoop to pick up Millie's discarded wrapping paper and the stranger moves towards me. There is a moment of jumbled arms and legs and then we are side by side.

welcome to the dance

On the carpet. Both clutching bits of sparkly wrapping paper.

"I don't know what to do," I say at last. "I don't know who you are."

She touches my face then. Hand so light, so tender I want it to go on forever.

"I'm sorry Saphy," she says at last and then I begin to cry.